ABRAHAM
LINCOLN

Deborah Kops

B L A C K B I R C H   P R E S S ,   I N C .

W O O D B R I D G E ,   C O N N E C T I C U T

For John

Published by Blackbirch Press, Inc.
260 Amity Road
Woodbridge, CT 06525
Web site: http://www.blackbirch.com
e-mail: staff@blackbirch.com
© 2001 Blackbirch Press, Inc.

Printed in China

10 9 8 7 6 5 4 3 2 1

Photo credits:
Cover: Blackbirch Press archives; cover (inset), pages 35, 39, 48, 60, 82: National Archives; pages 4, 6, 32, 36, 43, 56, 62, 90, 93, 96 (right), 97: ©North Wind Picture Archives; pages 9, 10, 13, 17, 25, 27, 46, 50-51, 52, 54, 55, 68, 70, 74, 78, 81, 87, 96 (left), 99: The Library of Congress; pages 18, 19, 22, 26, 33, 58: National Portrait Gallery; page 65: ©National Geographic; page 94: ©Bettman/Corbis; page 100: Bruce Glassman.

Library of Congress Cataloging-in-Publication Data
Kops, Deborah.
Abraham Lincoln / by Deborah Kops.
    p. cm. — (The Civil War)
Includes index.
    ISBN 1-56711-535-7
Summary: Focuses on the legal and political career of the self-educated man who led the United States during the Civil War, and looks at its effects on his wife and children.
1. Lincoln, Abraham, 1808–1865—Juvenile literature. 2. Presidents—United States—Biography—Juvenile literature. [1. Lincoln, Abraham, 1808–1865. 2. Presidents.] I. Title. II. Civil War (Blackbirch Press)
E457.905.K595 2001
973.7'092—dc21   2001002716

CONTENTS

Preface: The Civil War   4

Introduction:
    "It Is Hard to Have Him Die!"   8

Chapter 1   Living on the Frontier   11

Chapter 2   From Springfield to Washington   23

Chapter 3   Trial by Fire   53

Chapter 4   The Last Bloody Years   71

Chapter 5   Peace and Tragedy   83

Glossary   101

For More Information   102

Index   103

PREFACE: THE CIVIL WAR

Nearly 150 years after the final shots were fired, the Civil War remains one of the key events in U. S. history. The enormous loss of life alone makes it tragically unique: More Americans died in Civil War battles than in all other American wars combined. More Americans fell at the Battle of Gettysburg than during any battle in American military history. And, in one day at the Battle of Antietam, more Americans were killed and wounded than in any other day in American history.

As tragic as the loss of life was, however, it is the principles over which the war was fought that make it uniquely American. Those beliefs—equality and freedom—are the foundation of American democracy, our basic rights. It was the bitter disagreement about the exact nature of those rights that drove our nation to its bloodiest war.

The disagreements grew in part from the differing economies of the North and South. The warm climate and wide-open areas of the Southern states were ideal for an economy based on agriculture. In the first half of the

Slaves did the backbreaking work on Southern plantations.

19th century, the main cash crop was cotton, grown on large farms called plantations. Slaves, who were brought to the United States from Africa, were forced to do the backbreaking work of planting and harvesting cotton. They also provided the other labor necessary to keep plantations running. Slaves were bought and sold like property, and had been critical to the Southern economy since the first Africans came to America in 1619.

The suffering of African Americans under slavery is one of the great tragedies in American history. And the debate over whether the United States government had the right to forbid slavery—in both Southern states and in new territories—was a dispute that overshadowed the first 80 years of our history.

For many Northerners, the question of slavery was one of morality and not economics. Because the Northern economy was based on manufacturing rather than agriculture, there was little need for slave labor. The primary economic need of Northern states was a protective tax known as a tariff that would make imported goods more expensive than goods made in the North. Tariffs forced Southerners to buy Northern goods and made them economically dependent on the North, a fact that led to deep resentment among Southerners.

Economic control did not matter to the anti-slavery Northerners known as abolitionists. Their conflict with the South was over slavery. The idea that the federal government could outlaw slavery was perfectly reasonable. After all, abolitionists contended, our nation was founded on the idea that all people are created equal. How could slavery exist in such a country?

For the Southern states that joined the Confederacy, the freedom from unfair taxation and the right to make their

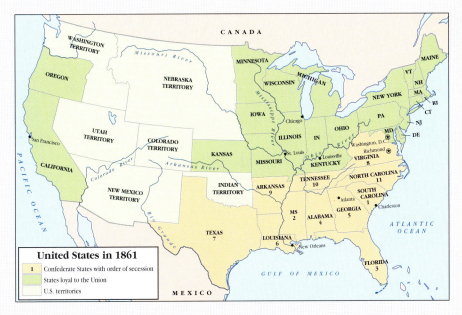

own decisions about slavery was as important a principle as equality. For most Southerners, the right of states to decide what is best for its citizens was the most important principle guaranteed in the Constitution.

The conflict over these principles generated sparks throughout the decades leading up to the Civil War. The importance of keeping an equal number of slave and free states in the Union became critical to Southern lawmakers in Congress in those years. In 1820, when Maine and Missouri sought admission to the Union, the question was settled by the Missouri Compromise: Maine was admitted as a free state, Missouri as a slave state, thus maintaining a balance in Congress. The compromise stated that all future territories north of the southern boundary of Missouri would enter the Union as free states, those south of it would be slave states.

In 1854, however, the Kansas-Nebraska Act set the stage for the Civil War. That act repealed the Missouri Compromise and by declaring that the question of slavery should be decided by residents of the territory, set off a rush of pro- and anti-slavery settlers to the new land. Violence between the two sides began almost immediately and soon "Bleeding Kansas" became a tragic chapter in our nation's story.

With Lincoln's election on an anti-slavery platform in 1860, the disagreement over the power of the federal government reached its breaking point. In early 1861, South Carolina became the first state to secede from the Union, followed by Mississippi, Florida, Alabama, Georgia, Louisiana, Virginia, Texas, North Carolina, Tennessee, and Arkansas. Those eleven states became the Confederate States of America. Confederate troops fired the first shots of the Civil War at Fort Sumter, South Carolina, on April 12, 1861. Those shots began a four-year war in which thousands of Americans—Northerners and Southerners—would give, in President Lincoln's words, "the last full measure of devotion."

OPPOSITE: The Confederate attack on Fort Sumter began the Civil War.

INTRODUCTION: "IT IS HARD TO HAVE HIM DIE!"

★ ★ ★ ★ ★

Late on a winter day in 1862, a tall, bearded, rail-thin man gazed sadly at an eleven-year-old boy lying in bed. The child's face was bright with fever; Abraham Lincoln knew his son Willie was near death. He'd seen typhoid all too often. Even now it claimed lives in Union army camps around the nation's capital.

The Lincoln family had lived at the White House for less than a year. During that time, Willie had gone to the camps to inspect the soldiers with his father. Willie and his younger brother, Tad, had also accompanied their mother, Mary, as she handed out gifts of fruit, books, and newspapers to the troops.

Though Lincoln deeply loved all of his children, everyone knew Willie was his favorite. The two were often seen walking the White House grounds hand-in-hand.

A few months before his illness struck, Willie and Tad had built a fort on the roof of the White House. While his father carried the weight of the Civil War on his shoulders, the boys had played war games, firing imaginary weapons.

The sickness had struck right after Christmas in 1861. Bright spots had appeared on the boy's abdomen, and he complained of back and neck pains. He lost his appetite and his energy. By February, Willie was weak and bedridden.

Today, we know that typhoid is caused by a bacteria in human waste. There are now vaccines to prevent typhoid, but in the 1800s, even being a president's son was not a guarantee of good health. Before doctors understood that germs caused disease, clean drinking water and proper waste treatment were as rare in the White House as they were on the battlefield.

Willie Lincoln was only 11 years old when he died from typhoid fever.

At 5:00 P.M. Willie Lincoln took his last breath with his parents at his bedside. A short time later, Lincoln would say, "My poor boy... was too good for this earth.... I know he is much better off in heaven, but then we loved him so. It is hard, hard to have him die!"

At that same time, civil war and disease were destroying many families and tearing the nation apart. Lincoln would eventually lose his own life while trying to hold the nation together, emerging as perhaps the nation's greatest president. On that day, however, Abraham Lincoln was simply a man with a broken heart whose beloved son had died.

Chapter 1

LIVING ON THE FRONTIER

Most Americans know some basic facts about Abraham Lincoln: he grew up in a log cabin, rose from his humble beginnings to become the president of the United States during the Civil War, and freed the slaves. Most also recognize Lincoln in photographs and paintings: his sad face with its high cheekbones, deep wrinkles, and short beard is one of the most recognizable of all American images. The man behind those easily recognized features, however, was far more complicated than most people realize.

OPPOSITE: Abraham Lincoln, raised in a one-room log cabin on the rugged frontier, grew up to become one of the greatest Americans.

11

Boyhood in a Cabin

Abraham Lincoln was born in northern Kentucky on February 12, 1809. At the age of two he moved with his parents, Thomas and Nancy Hanks Lincoln, and his older sister, Sarah, to a nearby farm where the land was more fertile. Their one-room log cabin was nestled among steep hills, called "knobs."

A neighbor remembered Lincoln as a "tall spider of a boy," and noted that he "had his due proportion of harmless mischief." Sometimes Abraham planted alongside his father. Thomas was a hard-working man who enjoyed swapping stories with his neighbors, a habit Lincoln soon adopted. His mother was quiet and very intelligent. Unlike her husband, she was able to read, an unusual skill for a woman of that time.

★

Jefferson Davis, future president of the Confederacy, was born two months before Lincoln, less than 10 miles away.

★

When Abraham was seven years old, the family crossed the Ohio River and settled in the new state of Indiana. Thomas had problems related to the legal ownership of his Kentucky land. In addition, he preferred to live in a state where slavery was illegal, because his Baptist religion taught him that enslaving another human being was wrong.

The Lincolns' new home, along Little Pigeon Creek in southern Indiana, was in a wilderness area with only a small community of settlers. Abraham quickly learned how to swing an ax. He spent his days helping his father with the exhausting work of clearing land for planting and enclosing it with split-rail fencing.

12

Life on the western frontier was dangerous, and days were filled with hard work.

Tragedy and Change

Frontier farms were different from modern farms that have picturesque barns and wide-open fields. The cows of the Little Pigeon Creek community grazed in the forests and ate what they pleased. Tragedy struck when the cows began eating snakeroot, a plant that did not kill them but made their milk poisonous to humans. Abraham's great aunt and uncle died of "milk sickness" first, and then his mother died from it in 1818, when young Abe was not quite ten years old.

The year that followed Nancy Lincoln's death was a gloomy one. Sarah, then twelve, struggled to handle the cooking, washing, and other work her mother had done. Life changed for the better, however, with the arrival of Thomas's new wife in

13

1819. Sarah Bush Lincoln had lost her husband and had three children—two girls and a boy—between the ages of thirteen and eight.

Abraham's stepmother was fair and loving to both sets of children, who got along well. She became especially fond of her tall stepson. "Abe never gave me a cross word or look and never refused . . . to do anything I requested him," she remembered later on. The boy adored her as well. He called her Mama and as an adult described her as his "best friend in the world."

On the frontier, schools were few and far between. Like many children, Abraham had little formal education—less than a year all together. When Abraham was a teenager, he managed to attend school for about nine months. His stepmother observed the way he went about teaching himself: "He must understand every thing—even to the smallest thing—minutely and exactly," she recalled. "He would then repeat it over to himself again and again . . . and when it was fixed in his mind to suit him . . . he never lost that fact or his understanding of it."

Abolitionists John Brown and Frederick Douglass both lost their mothers when they were children.

Abraham loved to read. *Aesop's Fables* and Parson Weems' *Life of Washington* were favorites. He would take a book with him when he plowed, and when he came to the end of a row, he would read while the horse rested. At home, he would grab a piece of cornbread and read some more.

At school, other students seemed to realize there was something special about the very tall boy with the buckskin pants that didn't reach his boots. They liked to gather around him and listen to his stories and jokes.

In 1830, the Lincoln family made one more move, this time to Illinois. Thomas Lincoln staked a claim to land on the banks of the Sangamon River in the center of the state. After spending a summer helping his father clear fields and fence them in, Abraham, 21, decided it was time to make his way in the world on his own. He wasn't ready to settle on an occupation, but he knew that he didn't want to continue the backbreaking work of a frontier farmer.

Politics Lures Young Lincoln

Lincoln's first job was to help build a flatbed boat for a man named Denton Offutt, load it with barrels of provisions, and sail it down the Mississippi River from Illinois to New Orleans. Offutt was impressed with Lincoln's intelligence and ingenuity. When the boat got hung up on a dam and became waterlogged, Lincoln bored a hole in the front, and unloaded enough barrels so that the rear end of the boat would rise. Water poured out the hole and the boat was saved.

After delivering the boat and cargo to New Orleans, Lincoln returned to New Salem, Illinois, to run a general store for Offutt. About twenty miles northwest of Springfield, New Salem was a commercial center for the surrounding farms.

15

Lincoln seemed to get along with everyone. It was impossible not to like the hard-working young man with an endless supply of jokes and stories.

Lincoln was interested in town affairs and often attended court sessions that were held by Bowling Green. New Salem's justice of the peace, Green encouraged Lincoln to publicly comment on cases because he was so amusing. But the justice soon realized that the long-legged young man was also very intelligent and encouraged Lincoln to run for the state legislature.

In March 1832, Lincoln announced his candidacy. He was only twenty-three years old and had been in New Salem less than a year. A political career was a good choice for an ambitious young man without money or family connections like Lincoln. Despite his popularity, his chances were slim The August election would be countywide, and the other candidates were older and more experienced. In the meantime, Lincoln took up the call of a different sort of battle. There was a war in northern Illinois.

Throughout the United States during those years, Native Americans had been forced to leave their tribal lands to make way for white settlers. Now, 450 Sauk and Fox warriors returned to Illinois to reclaim their home, led by Black Hawk. Lincoln signed up with the local militia to fight in what became known as the Black Hawk War. It was a valuable experience for the young candidate from New Salem because he met people from all regions of Illinois, some of whom became influential friends. He was very proud to be elected captain of his company, though he later poked fun at his only military experience: "I had a good many bloody struggles with the mosquitoes, and although I never fainted from loss of blood, I can truly say I was often very hungry."

An illustration of Black Hawk, who led the Sauk and Fox in an effort to reclaim tribal lands taken away by the U.S. government.

Lincoln lost the election in August, but he did very well in his hometown. Of the 300 votes cast in New Salem, he won 277. Now he badly needed work and jumped at the chance to become a partner with William Berry in a general store in New Salem. Berry had been a corporal in Lincoln's militia company.

17

Lincoln the Young Legislator

Business at the store was slow, and Lincoln spent a lot of time reading. He memorized long passages of Shakespeare and other poetry that appealed to him, and he taught himself grammar. When the store went out of business by the spring of 1833, Lincoln managed to get a modest position as postmaster of the town. To supplement his income, he studied advanced mathematics and became an assistant to the country surveyor for Sangamon.

In 1834, Lincoln made another run for the state legislature. Although it was not a presidential election year, voters were now identifying themselves more along party lines. Democrats were loyal to President Andrew Jackson and applauded his successful efforts at destroying the nation's powerful Bank of the United States so that local banks could have more control of "the people's" money. The new conservative Whig party was led by Jackson's enemy,

Andrew Jackson, hero of the War of 1812, was president in 1834. He was popular with the Democrats, especially for his banking policies.

Senator Henry Clay, who supported the federal bank and accused Jackson of acting more like a king than a president. Lincoln was a Whig and a great admirer of Clay, yet he remained popular with Democratic farmers as well as "Whiggish" villagers. He demonstrated his growing political skills by running a low-key campaign, chatting with residents all over Sangamon County—and keeping his political opinions to himself. On August 4, the young politician was finally elected to the legislature.

Henry Clay was a Whig and an outsopken critic of President Jackson's.

While he waited for his first session to begin in December, Lincoln decided to study law. Many lawyers in the country were self-taught, and he believed that the profession would provide him with a good income while helping his political career. John Todd Stuart, a young lawyer from Springfield and another young politician who also had won a legislative seat, offered to help. By the time Lincoln arrived in

19

the capital of Vandalia in his new suit, he had spent long hours studying Stuart's law books.

Vandalia was a prairie town of about 800 people. The statehouse, facing the town square, was a rundown, two-story brick building with the plaster falling from its ceilings. Comfortable with the language of the law, Lincoln gradually grew skilled at drafting legislation and even helped his colleagues.

When the session concluded in February, Lincoln pocketed $158 in salary—he'd already received $100—and returned to New Salem to study law with even greater determination. To support himself, he continued to survey property.

During the 1836 election, the Democrats staged a statewide political convention in the statehouse at Vandalia. Led by Stephen A. Douglas, they drafted a political platform and agreed to support all party candidates in the coming election, including Martin Van Buren for president. This new convention system angered the Whigs, who stood a better chance of winning the election if the Democrats were less unified.

★

The average worker's salary in the 1830s was about $250 per year.

★

Lincoln was prominent in the anti-convention fight, sometimes filling in as the Whig's floor leader for John Todd Stuart. At the close of the legislative session, Lincoln hit the campaign trail to run for re-election. He rode from town to town with other candidates,

Abraham Lincoln

speaking at public rallies and supporting the national Whig platform. In the November election, the Whigs swept Sangamon County, where Lincoln led the seven Whigs elected to the state legislature. There would also be two Whigs from the county in the Senate. All unusually tall men, they became known in the 1836-1837 session as the Long Nine.

The main goal of the Long Nine was the relocation of the state capital from sleepy Vandalia, in the southern part of the state, to Springfield, in Sangamon County. At the time, Illinois was growing rapidly as settlers from New York and New England streamed into its central region. As the population grew, it made sense that the seat of state government should be located there as well. Lincoln and his colleagues introduced a relocation bill that was approved only after a long and bitter fight.

At the close of the legislative session in 1837, Lincoln returned to New Salem to say goodbye to friends and pack. He was joining Stuart's law practice in Springfield. The twenty-eight-year-old lawyer had almost no money and would leave New Salem on a borrowed horse. He took great satisfaction, however, in all he had achieved. Lincoln had arrived in New Salem with a frontier farmer's skills and he was leaving as a legislator with a position in a Springfield law office.

★

In 1837, when Martin Van Buren took office as president, an economic panic hit the nation for the first time.

★

21

Chapter 2

In 1837, Springfield was still a crude frontier town. Hogs dug up the dirt roads, and when the wind blew a certain way, there was a disagreeable smell from stables and primitive outhouses. Compared to New Salem, however, Springfield was civilized. There were four hotels, two newspapers, and soon a new statehouse. For an ambitious young man like Lincoln, Springfield was an interesting place.

OPPOSITE: Lincoln was a successful lawyer in Springfield, Illinois, in the 1850s.

23

The law firm of Stuart & Lincoln was a busy one. Lincoln often appeared before the Sangamon County Circuit Court in Springfield when it was in session, which was only four weeks out of the year. At other times, Lincoln would ride the circuit, arguing cases before circuit courts in other counties. Although most cases were routine, Lincoln handled some exciting criminal cases, including a murder trial. Hardworking as always, he gradually mastered the technical aspects of his work. Keeping records, however, was another matter. He set papers down, absent-mindedly, in all sorts of odd places, including his tall stovepipe hat.

The year 1838 was an election year for Lincoln and for his partner, who was running against Stephen Douglas for U.S. representative. While traveling the circuit, Lincoln campaigned for Stuart. At the same time, he worked hard to help organize the Whig party, becoming a prominent leader himself in the process. Lincoln won his election easily, but Stuart had a tough fight, and defeated Douglas by only a small margin.

In the next session of the legislature, Lincoln fought hard for continued improvement programs for Illinois, including railroads and canals. These would be a challenge for the state to finance, however, because like other states, Illinois had been badly shaken by a financial panic that had swept the nation in 1837. Lincoln also led the Whigs in a fight to support the State Bank of Illinois, a frequent target of Democratic attacks.

By the fall of 1839, Lincoln and his fellow Whigs began organizing for the coming presidential election in 1840. Both Lincoln and Stuart were again up for re-election. In October, the Whigs held a

Martin Van Buren ran for re-election in 1840 on the Democratic ticket.

Abraham Lincoln

William Henry Harrison won the election of 1840, but died after only two months in office.

convention in Springfield and gave military hero William Henry Harrison their support in his run against Martin Van Buren, the Democratic candidate.

During the campaign, Stephen Douglas, chairman of the Democratic state committee, challenged Lincoln to debate the principles of the two opposing parties. It was the first public debate for Lincoln and Douglas, who were destined to become lifelong rivals. Although the young legislator thought Douglas had gotten the better of him, most people thought it was a draw.

On the Home Front

Although Lincoln was becoming an accomplished speaker and was very entertaining in the company of men, he felt shy and tongue-tied around women. At age thirty, he was still unattached. Ninian and Elizabeth Edwards, a socially prominent couple at Springfield, introduced Lincoln to many single women at the fashionable parties they gave in their hilltop mansion. It was Elizabeth's sister, Mary Todd, however, who captured his heart.

Mary Todd was very pretty, with light brown hair, and lively blue eyes. Lincoln told her he would like to dance with her "in the worst way." Mary, teasingly turned his request into a comment on his dancing, and later noted that he did, in fact, dance in the "worst way."

Standing together, they illustrated the old saying that opposites attract. Unlike the long-legged Springfield lawyer, Mary was plump and short. Born into a wealthy family in Kentucky, she was much more skilled at social conversation than Lincoln, which greatly impressed him. The two also shared many interests. Although women could not vote, Mary was interested in politics and considered herself a Whig. Like Lincoln, she loved poetry. Since Mary was in Springfield on a long visit, Lincoln had many opportunities to call on her. By December 1840, they were engaged.

A stormy two years followed. Lincoln became anxious about their forthcoming marriage, called it off, and then became so depressed it was difficult for him to work. The happy marriage of his good friend Joshua Speed, however, greatly encouraged Lincoln. On November 4, 1842, Mary and Lincoln were married at the Edwards' home. In a driving rain, they rode from the mansion to the single room at the Globe Tavern where they would live.

Mary Todd met Lincoln in 1840 and married him two years later.

27

The Lincolns' first child was born on August 1, 1843. They named him Robert Todd, after Mary's father. The next year they bought a small house with three rooms downstairs and two bedrooms in the half loft, where the ceilings sloped so much that Lincoln had little room to stand up.

Finding the Right Partner

In the first years of his family life, Lincoln struggled to earn a good living. He and Stuart had dissolved their business because Stuart was in Washington much of the time. Instead Lincoln formed a partnership with Stephen T. Logan, a fellow Whig leader and former judge, who was a successful attorney in Springfield. Determined to match that success, Lincoln focused his enormous capacity for hard work on their law practice. Business was good, and the partners moved to new quarters, where they took on an assistant, Billy Herndon, a law student.

Nine years older than his partner, Logan was a small man with a shrill voice who did not make a good impression on juries. He thought Lincoln would do better, and he was right. As a county surveyor and state legislator, Lincoln knew a lot of people. He seemed to be acquainted with almost everyone who sat before him on a jury. His ability to communicate complicated thoughts simply and directly, which later made him a powerful orator, made him very effective during closing arguments.

28

Although Lincoln was smooth and accomplished in court, he was, and would always be, an awkward figure. With only 160 pounds on his six-foot four-inch frame, he was very thin, which made him look even taller than he was, with long legs out of proportion to his body. Photos of Lincoln back up Billy Herndon's detailed description of him: "His hair was dark—almost black—and lay floating where the fingers or the winds left it, piled up at random. His eyebrows cropped out like a huge rock on the brow of a hill. His cheeks were leathery and flabby, falling in loose folds in places, looking sorrowful."

Eventually, Logan and Lincoln dissolved their partnership. Lincoln turned to Billy Herndon. "Billy," he said, "I can trust you, if you can trust me." Lincoln thought the young man showed a lot of promise, and the two developed a warm and successful partnership.

Back on the Campaign Trail

Lincoln's law practice absorbed much of his time, but he also remained keenly interested in politics. In 1844, he campaigned for Henry Clay, the Whig candidate for president, and he also stumped enthusiastically and successfully for his friend Edward Baker, a candidate for the U.S. House of Representatives. Lincoln, however, was not acting selflessly. Baker promised that when his term was over, he would not run again, and Lincoln would be next in line.

29

In May 1846, Lincoln became the Whig candidate for state representative. His Democratic opponent, Peter Cartwright, was not a strong campaigner. A devout Methodist, he accused Lincoln of not having any faith. His charge didn't seem to damage Lincoln, who denied the accusation and beat him easily. He would now represent his district in the Thirtieth Congress, which would meet in Washington in December 1847. In the meantime, he could become better acquainted with his second son, Eddie, born in March.

The 1846 elections focused on the disputes that had led to the Mexican-American War. The United States had become involved in a border dispute between Mexico and the new state of Texas. After minor fighting between Mexican and American forces, President James Polk declared war. Lincoln allowed himself to get caught up in the patriotic war fever, but he had private doubts about whether the war was justified. When the war ended in 1848, the United States gained more than one million square miles of territory in what are now the states of California, Arizona, Nevada, Utah, New Mexico, and Colorado.

The acquisition of new land intensified the bitter disagreement over slavery, and whether or not it should be allowed to spread. For more than twenty-five years, the Missouri Compromise, which prohibited slavery above the southern border of Missouri, has been used to determine whether an area would be slave or free. Many Southern lawmakers, however, wanted to revoke the compromise, fearing that most new territory that came into the Union would be north of Missouri's southern border.

Those who were against slavery worried that the enormous size of territories such as Texas could mean that the area would be divided into many smaller states—all of which permitted slavery. This would upset the balance in Congress and allow slavery to continue.

Many lawmakers who had no strong feelings about the question shared Lincoln's view that if slavery was not allowed to spread, it would eventually die out altogether. Those who shared that view, however, would soon be forced to choose one side or the other in the bitter debate.

Congressman Lincoln

The Lincoln family arrived in Washington on December 2, 1847. The nation's capital was then a bustling city of 40,000 people, including 2,000 slaves and 8,000 free African Americans. But Mary and the boys soon found lodging at Mrs. Sprigg's boardinghouse too confining. After three months in the city, they left to stay with Mary's father in Kentucky.

The freshman representative from Springfield was the only Whig from Illinois in the House. Lincoln was disappointed to find his fellow Whigs from other states disorganized and worried about

31

losing the 1848 presidential election. When President James Polk, a Democrat, asked for additional funds to fight the war with Mexico, the Whigs went on the attack. They accused Polk of starting the war without justification. Lincoln challenged Polk to prove that the spot where American blood was first shed was actually U.S. soil. Unfortunately, the Whigs accomplished little in this skirmish with the president, who never bothered to reply to their charges. And the freshman from Illinois earned the nickname "Spotty Lincoln" and some unfavorable comments from journalists who found his speeches unpatriotic.

Though the Whigs criticized Polk for starting the Mexican-American War, they nominated one

The Battle of San Gabriel, California, helped the U.S. take control of territory held by Mexico during the Mexican-American War.

of the war's military heroes, General Zachary Taylor, for president. This practical, though not very idealistic, strategy worked. Lincoln campaigned hard for Taylor, who won his race against the Democrat Lewis Cass and the candidate of the anti-slavery Free Soil Party, former president Martin Van Buren.

In December 1848, Lincoln returned for his final congressional session. During his campaign, he had pledged that he would only

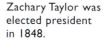

Zachary Taylor was elected president in 1848.

hold office for one term—the same promise he had extracted from the previous congressman from his district, Edward Baker.

Slavery became the dominant issue in Congress. In the previous session, Lincoln had supported Pennsylvanian David Wilmot's proposal to exclude slavery from any lands won from Mexico during the war. But he did not participate in the bitter debates over what became known as the Wilmot Proviso, which did not pass.

Now, frustrated antislavery congressmen took a new approach. They tried to outlaw slavery in Washington, D.C. Only seven blocks from the Capitol was a warehouse belonging to the nation's

33

largest slave trader. The anti-slavery forces thought the warehouse, and slavery itself, were a disgrace in a country that celebrated liberty. Lincoln agreed, but remained quiet. In Washington, however, he voted against measures to outlaw slavery. He thought only a proposal that came from the actual residents of Washington, D.C. should be approved. In May, when the congressional session was over, Lincoln went home.

The Return to Springfield

For the next five years, Lincoln turned his back on politics and concentrated on his law practice. It did not take long for Lincoln & Herndon to return to their old level of activity. Once again, Lincoln traveled the Eighth Circuit, this time in the company of Judge David Davis. The judge, a very heavy, but always neatly dressed man, was impressed with Lincoln's honesty and skill, though probably not with his court attire, which sometimes included a shawl fastened with a large safety pin. However, in December 1849, Lincoln was needed at home. Eddie had become very sick with tuberculosis and died two months later. The Lincolns were devastated. Mary soon became pregnant again and gave birth to William, a very bright and sensitive child who quickly found a tender place in his father's affections. Then, in 1853, Thomas, the last child, was born. He had a large head as a baby, which reminded his parents of a tadpole's, and they nicknamed him "Tad."

By the time Tad was born, a network of railroads was spreading across Illinois. Their growth pleased Lincoln for a number of reasons. He thought they would help the state's economy, and in the meantime, they would create a great deal of interesting and high-paying legal work to build his reputation. The railroads also provided Lincoln with a faster way to get home when he was traveling the circuit, which meant he could return on weekends.

Mary felt very burdened by the long hours she spent alone with her boys, so Lincoln sometimes cared for the two younger ones to give her a rest. He would pull Willie and Tad around in a wagon with one hand while holding a book in the other. On at least one occasion, he became so absorbed

Lincoln shares one of his favorite pastimes with his youngest son, Tad.

in his book that he didn't notice that a child had fallen out of the wagon.

The Slavery Question

In 1854, Lincoln finally left the political sidelines after the passage of the Kansas-Nebraska Act, a controversial piece of legislation that was approved largely through the efforts of Stephen A. Douglas, now a U.S. senator from Illinois. The act divided an enormous plains region into two territories, Kansas and Nebraska. Both territories were north of the southern border of Missouri, and would, under the 1820 Missouri Compromise, enter the Union as free states. Again, balance became an issue in Congress.

Senator Stephen Douglas of Illinois supported the interests of the South. He was a key figure in the passage of the Kansas-Nebraska Act.

In order to gain Southern support for an act that would allow the territories to enter the Union, Douglas got rid of the Missouri Compromise that had dealt with the slavery question for thirty-four years. Douglas's efforts on behalf of the act, however, had little to do with slavery.

At that time, plans were being drawn up for rail lines to be laid from a Midwestern city to the

Pacific Ocean. Douglas hoped to make Chicago, Illinois, one end of the first transcontinental railroad. Before a company would lay tracks west from Chicago, however, it had to be assured that the lands would eventually become states under federal power.

Douglas wanted to admit all lands west of Missouri as states, so he added an important amendment to the Kansas-Nebraska Act. The amendment overruled the Missouri Compromise and replaced it with the law stating that the question of slavery would be settled by a vote of the residents of the territory rather than by the federal government. That amendment guaranteed the passage of the act.

The Kansas-Nebraska bill also laid out the rules for setting up the first elections and gave every advantage to slaveholders and supporters. The Fugitive Slave Laws of 1850 were in effect in the territory, meaning that anti-slavery people who helped slaves escape could themselves be jailed and thus unable to vote. Many anti-slavery voters, such as U.S. soldiers, who made up much of Kansas' population, were specifically excluded from the vote.

The Kansas-Nebraska Act, signed into law on May 30, 1854, was a huge success for the South. The North, on the other hand, viewed the Kansas-Nebraska Act as a betrayal. Most Northerners refused to accept it. Instead, many threw their support behind a new political party, the Republican

Party, which was in favor of new rail lines, free land in the West—and strongly opposed to slavery.

A storm of protest raged in the North. Northern Whigs and Northern Democrats all opposed the act. Violence between pro- and anti-slavery forces soon broke out in Kansas. Abolitionist John Brown led a raid on pro-slavery settlers that killed five men. Soon the territory became known as "Bleeding Kansas."

The bitter disagreements and violence began to pull the traditional parties—and the nation—apart. When Douglas came through Illinois to drum up support for the Democrats in the 1854 elections while defending the Kansas-Nebraska Act, Lincoln decided to challenge him. The opening of the Illinois State Fair in Springfield was the perfect opportunity. On October 3, Douglas spoke in the state House of Representatives. The next day, Lincoln gave his rebuttal.

It was a dramatic speech in which Lincoln spelled out many of the beliefs that later guided him during his presidency. He argued that the Constitution did not permit Congress to outlaw slavery in states where it was permitted by state law. But, Lincoln said, according to the Constitution, Congress could bar slavery from new territories. And for moral reasons, he continued, slavery should not be allowed to spread. The Declaration of Independence stated that all men were created equal, and slavery was a violation of this principle. "No man," Lincoln boomed, "is good enough to govern another man without that man's consent." He pointed out that Douglas did not seem to recognize that African Americans were human beings who deserved the protection of the law.

Lincoln spoke for three hours on that hot and humid afternoon. The antislavery forces in the region were thrilled with the speech. A small group immediately called a meeting to organize the Illinois branch of the new Republican Party. Although Lincoln was invited to be a member of a central committee, he wasn't ready to identify himself as a Republican. Lincoln had his eye on the U.S. Senate, and could not afford to lose the support of the Whigs.

Abolitionist John Brown led a raid on pro-slavery settlers in Kansas after the passage of the Kansas-Nebraska Act.

Joining the Republicans

Much to Lincoln's delight, the results of the 1854 election showed that many "anti-Nebraska" candidates—those opposed to the Kansas-Nebraska Act in Illinois—were winners. This was true in other Northern states as well. At that time, voters did not elect senators directly; they were elected by the state legislature. Lincoln set about trying to win supporters for the January 1855 election.

39

The attorney from Springfield proved very skilled at political maneuvering, but he did not have quite enough votes to win. Once he realized this, he instructed his supporters to vote for Lyman Trumbull, an anti-Nebraska Democrat, who won the race as a result. Trumbull's supporters declared that they would back Lincoln for the next senate race in 1858.

In 1856, a serious effort was made to organize a Republican Party in Illinois, and this time, Lincoln was one of its organizers. He realized that the Whig party was no longer a strong political force in the country. Lincoln gave a fiery speech to wrap up a convention in May that officially established the Republicans in Illinois. He declared the party's opposition to the expansion of slavery and acknowledged that some Southerners might want to leave the Union rather than agree with this policy. To them he repeated the famous words of Daniel Webster, "Liberty and Union, now and forever, one and inseparable." They became the motto of the Republican Party.

That spring, while Lincoln was helping to build a new Republican Party, his house on the corner of Eighth and Jackson Streets was being expanded. He was earning enough money that he and Mary could finally afford some much-needed space. Their small home was soon transformed into a handsome, two-story house painted chocolate brown and trimmed with green shutters.

★

In 1856, Robert E. Lee freed his slaves and called slavery "a moral and political evil."

★

"A House Divided"

Late in the summer of 1857, Lincoln and his supporters began to organize for the November 1858 state elections. Because state legislators would elect the U.S. senator, the 1858 election was crucial because it would decide who most of those legislators would be.

When the Republican state convention met in Springfield on June 16, 1858, Lincoln's friends came prepared to nominate him as the party's candidate for U.S. senator. A Chicago delegation brought in their banner that read, "Cook County is for Abraham Lincoln." Then a delegate from Peoria interrupted the applause to suggest that the banner read "The State of Illinois is for Abraham Lincoln." The delegates went wild and unanimously elected Lincoln as their candidate.

That night, Lincoln gave a powerful acceptance speech with ringing words that are among his best known. Speaking of the Kansas-Nebraska Act he said,

> We are now into the fifth year, since a policy was initiated with the avowed object, and confident promise, of putting an end to slavery agitation. Under the operation of that policy that agitation has not only, not ceased, but has constantly augmented.
>
> In my opinion, it will not cease, until a crisis shall have been reached, and passed. A house divided against itself cannot stand. I believe this government cannot endure, permanently half slave and half free.

41

The Lincoln-Douglas Debates

In July 1858, Lincoln invited Douglas to appear with him in a series of public debates, and Douglas reluctantly agreed. There were seven all together, each in a different region of Illinois. Thousands of people arrived by foot, horseback, or carriage to attend these debates, which remain the most famous in American history. People sat outside for hours in the summer heat or pouring rain to hear the two men argue about slavery. It was the burning issue of the day, and the debates received national attention.

Lincoln and Douglas took turns giving the opening one-hour speech. It was followed by a one-and-a-half hour reply by the second speaker, and then closing remarks by the first. Side by side, they were a strange pair. Lincoln looked as tall and rail-thin as ever. Douglas was stout and reached only to Lincoln's shoulders.

The strategy of the first speaker was to aggressively attack his opponent on an issue that would reveal his weakness. Lincoln accused Douglas of ignoring the Declaration of Independence and the Constitution. He argued that the Founders thought slavery was wrong and wanted to prevent it from spreading. Instead, Douglas was trying to make it a national institution. He was, Lincoln said, "blowing out the moral lights around us."

Douglas replied that the Constitution left it up to the states to permit slavery or not. He attacked Lincoln's argument that the principle of equality

42

The Lincoln-Douglas debates were held across Illinois during the summer of 1858.

spelled out in the Declaration of Independence applied to African Americans. Douglas knew that most people in Illinois, even those opposed to slavery, were prejudiced against African Americans. He played on these prejudices by claiming that Lincoln thought African American men should be allowed to vote and even to marry whites. Lincoln denied these claims.

In truth, he was not completely free of prejudice himself. He stated forcefully, however, that "in the right to eat the bread, without leave [permission] of anybody else, which his own hand earns [a black person] is my equal and the equal of Judge Douglas, and the equal of every living man."

In the long view of history, Lincoln won the debates. Although the Republicans did not gain enough seats in the state legislature to vote him the next senator from Illinois, he was now a nationally known figure on the political stage.

Thoughts of the White House

Lincoln continued to speak publicly against the expansion of slavery into the territories and was warmly received. To anyone who suggested he run for president, however, he replied that he wasn't qualified. His political experience was, in fact, very limited. He had only served one term in Congress, and the Illinois legislature did not prepare a person for the presidency. As for administrative experience, Lincoln didn't have any—not beyond managing a two-person law office. He remained an ambitious man, however, and soon began to consider the 1860 presidential election more seriously.

An invitation to speak in New York City in February 1860 presented a great opportunity for Lincoln to gain publicity in the heavily populated East Coast, which was an important region during presidential elections. In addition, New York was the territory of the leading contender for the Republican nomination, the senator and former governor, William Seward. On February 27, a snowstorm pounded New York City. Despite the weather, 1,500 people listened to Lincoln speak inside the great hall of Cooper Union, a new architecture and engineering school.

Lincoln gave an inspired, well-thought-out speech in which he attempted to prove that the Founders meant to exclude slavery from new territories. He urged Republicans to continue along that path despite any opposition. He concluded with the stirring words, "Let us have faith that right makes might, and in that faith, let us, to the end, dare to do our duty as we understand it." The crowd cheered and waved their hats. Journalists were equally enthusiastic the next day. Horace Greeley, founder and editor of the influential *New York Tribune*, proclaimed Lincoln, "one of Nature's orators." He was now among the front-runners for the Republican nomination for president.

Lincoln the Rail Splitter

Lincoln and his supporters realized that he would not be the first choice of most delegates to the Republican convention of 1860. He was, after all, still unknown in some parts of the country. If Seward did not get enough votes on the first ballot, however, Lincoln might have a chance—but so would the other Republican candidates. The

45

In 1860, Lincoln rose to national prominence as a leading contender for the Republican presidential nomination.

strategy was to get unanimous support for Lincoln's candidacy from the Illinois Republican delegates.

When the state party met in Decatur in May, one week before the national convention, Lincoln's campaign managers were ready. The delegates were assembled in a large, open-air, building that western Republicans used for their conventions. Down the aisle marched Lincoln's elderly relative, John Hanks, and an assistant carrying two log rails that Lincoln had helped split long ago. They were decorated with streamers and labeled

ABRAHAM LINCOLN
The Rail Candidate
FOR PRESIDENT IN 1860
Two rails from a lot of 3,000 made in 1830 by Thos.
Hanks and Abe Lincoln—whose father was the
first pioneer of Macon County.

The audience cheered, and the next day they instructed their delegates to the Republican national convention to vote unanimously for Lincoln. The candidate from Springfield became known as Lincoln "the Rail Splitter." People liked the image of a plain speaking, honest man making the trip from a frontier log cabin all the way to the presidency. Thirty years earlier, Andrew Jackson, "Old Hickory," had used the same approach to win the presidency.

47

The Rally in Chicago

The Republican national convention took place between May 16 and 18 in Chicago. The stakes for the presidential nomination were very high. A month before, Democrats had been unable to agree on one candidate, and it seemed likely the party would split in two at its next meeting in Baltimore. If that occurred, it was likely that the Republican candidate would win the presidency.

Lincoln did not attend the convention, and he was in his office when a reporter for the *Illinois State Journal* came in with the results of the first ballot: Seward received 173 1/2, which was 60 votes short of the 233 needed for his nomination. Lincoln polled 102, a very good first showing, and the remaining three candidates received about 50 each. The Springfield nominee was very encouraged and walked over to the telegraph office to get the

William Seward lost the Republican presidential nomination to Lincoln at the convention of 1860.

results of the next ballot: Seward rose to 184 1/2, but Lincoln now had 181. He awaited the third ballot in the *Journal's* office. The supporters of the three losing candidates had switched their votes, and Lincoln secured the nomination.

The next month, in Baltimore, the Democrats had another bitter meeting. Unable to reach an agreement with the Northerners, the Southerners nominated Vice President John C. Breckinridge of Kentucky, who was then serving under President James Buchanan. The Northern Democrats nominated Stephen Douglas. Yet another party, the pro-slavery Constitutional Unionists, nominated a Tennessee slaveholder, John Bell.

Election Day

In the months before the November election, Lincoln spent a lot of time answering letters of congratulations on his nomination and obliging requests for his autographs. He went along with tradition and did not campaign on behalf of his ticket, which included Hannibal Hamlin, a former Democrat from Maine, chosen by the convention to be his vice presidential running mate. Thousands of Republicans, however, held rallies and marched in parades carrying the fence rails that symbolized his campaign. Douglas broke with custom and campaigned for himself, crossing the entire country and speaking until he was hoarse.

Southerners were furious at the thought of a victory for Lincoln, which they knew would probably spell the end of slavery. A newspaper in Georgia declared, "Let the consequences be what they may—whether the Potomac is crimsoned in human gore, and Pennsylvania Avenue is paved ten fathoms deep with mangled bodies....the South

49

On November 6, 1860, the Lincoln-Hamlin ticket swept to victory. Overcoming his relative lack of political experience, Lincoln and his supporters had crafted an effective campaign that portrayed him as an honest, hard-working, and humble man from a simple pioneer background.

FREE SPEECH, FREE HOMES, FREE TERRITORY.

FOR PRESIDENT
ABRAHAM LINCOLN
OF ILLINOIS.

PROTECTION TO AMERICAN INDUSTRY

will never submit to such humiliation and degradation as the inauguration of Abraham Lincoln."

November 6 was the nation's general election day. That evening, Lincoln waited for the results at the capital with other Republicans. He was doing well in the Midwest and in the West, but awaited

FOR VICE PRESIDENT
ANNIBAL HAMLIN
OF MAINE

news of the crucial eastern states. At 10 P.M., accounts of Republican victories in Pennsylvania started coming in. After a late dinner at Watson's Saloon, Lincoln wandered over to the telegraph office. Finally, at 2 A.M., he learned that he had won New York and the presidency would be his. Later he remembered, "I went home, but I did not sleep, for I then felt as I never had before, the responsibility that was upon me."

In the four months before his inauguration, Lincoln faced a constant stream of people looking for federal jobs. Lincoln also received a large amount of hate mail. The day before his departure for Washington, D.C., Lincoln stopped at his old law office and told his partner to leave the Lincoln & Herndon shingle up. Some day, he told Billy, he planned to continue practicing law.

51

Chapter 3

TRIAL BY FIRE

On February 11, 1861, Lincoln said good-bye to a crowd of people gathered at the railroad station in Springfield. Many were neighbors and friends, and Lincoln was very moved to see them all. "My friends," he said, "no one . . . can appreciate my feeling of sadness at this parting. To this place, and the kindness of these people, I owe everything. Here I have lived a quarter of a century, and have passed from a young to an old man. Here my children have been born and one is buried. I now leave, not knowing when, or whether ever, I may return."

OPPOSITE PAGE: Lincoln's inaugural procession made its way down Pennsylvania Avenue in Washington, D.C, on March 4, 1861.

Abraham Lincoln

By the time Lincoln left Illinois, six Southern states had already left the Union. South Carolina seceded first and was followed by Florida, Mississippi, Alabama, Georgia, Louisiana, and Texas. By the time Lincoln arrived in Washington, Jefferson Davis was the president of the Confederate States of America.

President-Elect Lincoln

All along the route people came out to catch a glimpse of their new president, as well as Mary and the boys, who accompanied him on most of the ride. He would appear on the train platform in the back so that, he explained with his characteristic humor, "I may see you and that you may see me, and in the arrangement I have the best of the bargain." Sometimes bands played and cannons fired. In Columbus, Ohio, 60,000 people stood in the damp chill to hear Lincoln speak. By the end of

The Capitol Building was not yet finished when Lincoln took office in 1861.

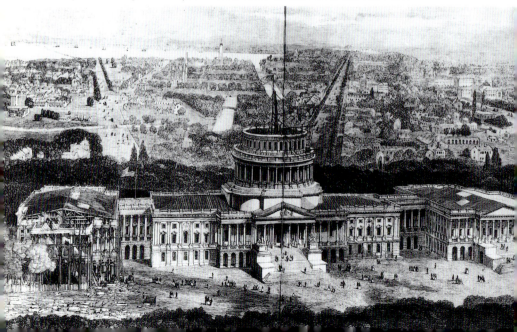

the trip, Mary Lincoln was comfortable enough to occasionally stand beside her husband. For the boys, the trip was a great adventure. Robert tried to drive the train once. Tad and Willie amused themselves by mischievously asking visitors who boarded the train if they would like to see "Old Abe." Then they would point out someone else in the train.

Hannibal Hamlin was Lincoln's vice president.

Washington was dirtier than it had been when Lincoln was a congressman. There were marshes filled with sewage, and the long, green mall near the Capitol was strewn with garbage. On a rise above the mall, a shaft of white marble rose toward the sky—a planned monument for George Washington. The family checked into the Willard Hotel, where they would stay until Inauguration Day, March 4, 1861.

Lincoln had made the final selection of his cabinet members the week before. He wanted men who would help him unite the country behind his administration, and also provide some of the experience in government that he lacked. Four of his choices were his main rivals for the Republican nomination for president: William Seward became secretary of state; Edward Bates, a Missouri lawyer, agreed to be attorney general; and Salmon P. Chase, the former Ohio governor, accepted the

Secretary of the Treasury Salmon P. Chase supported tough treatment for states that seceded.

post of secretary of the treasury. In addition, Lincoln appointed Gideon Welles secretary of the Navy; Simon Cameron, a senator from Pennsylvania, secretary of war; and Montgomery Blair, a Republican from Maryland, postmaster general. Cameron was the most controversial choice. Lincoln chose him after being showered with letters of support for Cameron. Others, however, accused Cameron of bribery and worse.

Problems with the cabinet began immediately. Chase spoke out bluntly against the secessionists. Seward wanted to avoid angering the South in the hopes it would rejoin the Union. When Lincoln chose Chase for the treasury, Seward threatened to resign. Lincoln handled him with diplomatic skill, and his first cabinet crisis was quickly resolved.

Clouds threatened a downpour on Inauguration Day. To everyone's relief, by the time Lincoln took the traditional carriage ride down Pennsylvania Avenue with President James Buchanan, the sun shone. Rising to stand on a large podium in front of the capitol, Lincoln was unsure of what to do with his tall stovepipe hat. His old rival, Stephen Douglas, noticed his confusion and graciously offered to hold it.

The new president promised to defend the Union. He assured Southerners that the government would not use violence unless forced to, but would "hold, occupy, and possess" government forts that lay within the borders of the Confederate states. He was thinking of Fort Sumter, in particular. When a ship had tried to bring troops and supplies to Fort Sumter in January, South Carolinians fired on it, forcing it to retreat. At Seward's urging, Lincoln ended his address with a plea for peace: "I am loathe to close. We are not enemies," he said, "but friends. We must not be enemies. Though passion may have strained, it must not break our bonds of affection."

War!

The next day, Lincoln found a troubling report on his desk. Major Robert Anderson, the commander of Fort Sumter, warned that in six weeks he would run out of supplies, including food. Lincoln did not react immediately. He was a cautious leader. By April 6, he had finally made up his mind. He informed Francis Pickens, the governor of South Carolina, that he was going to resupply the fort with food, but not with arms. For protection, he planted warships outside Charleston's harbor. It was a masterful plan: If the Confederates fired on the supply boat, they would be guilty of aggression, and of starting the war. If they allowed the fort to be supplied, the Union would win a symbolic victory.

On April 12 at 4:30 A.M., before the supply boats had arrived, the Confederate commander in Charleston, under orders from Jefferson Davis, told gunners to fire on the fort. The Union warships, scattered by a storm, were unable to help the men at the fort. After nearly two days of bombardment, Major Anderson surrendered. None of his men had been killed by enemy fire, but the Civil War had begun. Lincoln immediately called for 75,000 white men from state militias to put down the rebellion. (African Americans were not welcomed into the army until later.) Within less than a month, Virginia, Arkansas, North Carolina, and Tennessee joined the Confederacy.

Jefferson Davis was the president of the Confederate States.

A wave of patriotic enthusiasm washed over the North. Everyone seemed relieved that the waiting was over and the war had finally arrived. *The Chicago Tribune* predicted the Union would win in two or three months. *The New York Times*, even more optimistic, predicted victory in a month. Lincoln was more realistic. "Man for man," he pointed out, "the soldier from the South will be a match for the soldier from the North and vice versa."

The Union's general-in-chief was seventy-four-year-old Winfield Scott, a hero of the Mexican War. Scott wanted to gradually seal off the South by blockading its port cities along the coast and sending a fleet of gunboats down the Mississippi River. His plan would take time, and the public was impatient for action.

Lincoln, too, decided it was time to act. He ordered General Irvin McDowell, commander of the Union troops in Washington, to lead an advance against 20,000 Confederate troops assembled in Manassas, Virginia, a railroad junction near the Bull Run River. Another 11,000 Confederates were guarding the federal arsenal in nearby Harpers Ferry, which they had taken over in April. Stationed in the same vicinity were 15,000 Union men under the command of Major General Robert Patterson, a sixty-nine-year-old veteran of the War of 1812. For the Union forces to win, it was essential that Patterson prevent the Confederates at Harpers Ferry from reinforcing the rebels in Manassas.

The battle, called the Battle of Bull Run in the North and the Battle of Manassas in the South, began early on Sunday, July 21. By 6 P.M., Seward went to the White House to tell Lincoln that the Union forces had lost and were retreating toward Washington.

Bull Run was not a crucial battle in terms of military strategy. It was the first battle, however, and the Union's loss was a severe blow. Within days, Lincoln called for one million more volunteers. He appointed the handsome and energetic George B. McClellan to build an army out of the

A soldier sits near a railroad bridge that crosses over the Bull Run River, scene of the first battle of the Civil War.

men who were soon pouring into the training camps near Washington. It would be known as the Army of the Potomac.

In the White House

While McClellan trained his army, Lincoln took care of routine matters. With the help of his secretary John Nicolay and Nicolay's assistant, John Hay, he tried to handle the 200 to 300 letters that arrived daily. Lincoln, however, was more interested in seeing his visitors. From dawn until dusk people waited outside Lincoln's office to apply for a job or military appointment, or to get help with some problem. The president saw as many people as he could. Although most of them wanted favors, they also gave Lincoln an idea of how people felt about his administration. He jokingly referred to his office hours as "public opinion baths."

Stories about Lincoln's great patience and sympathy got around. In appreciation, supporters showered him and his family with presents: overcoats, canes, and hand-knitted socks for the president, New England salmon for the presidential pantry, and pet goats and rabbits for the children.

Willie and Tad adored their two goats—Nanko and Nanny. Tad once tied Nanko to a chair and went on a wild ride through the East Room during a reception. When Lincoln could spare a few minutes, he played with them. One visitor was amused to find the president on his back, pinned down by two of his sons and their friends.

The McClellan Problem

By the fall of 1861, the public grew impatient with McClellan. He had done a masterful job of reorganizing and training the army, and it was time, many thought, for an offensive against the Rebels. On October 21, McClellan obliged by sending 1,700 of his men across the Potomac to push the Confederates out of Leesburg, Virginia, about forty miles from Washington. The inexperienced Union soldiers chose their positions poorly, and over half were killed, wounded, or captured. In Congress, critics blamed McClellan for the humiliating loss. He in turn blamed Winfield Scott. Congress then pressured Lincoln to remove the aged general from his command. Lincoln did so with great regret, appointing McClellan general-in-chief of the army.

61

The War Department was another focus of congressional dissatisfaction, and with good reason. Manufacturers of shoddy equipment for the army—rotten blankets, knapsacks that fell apart, and other items—were making fortunes. Secretary of War Simon Cameron managed to antagonize everyone and was mistrusted by the public. Lincoln was advised that if he wanted cooperation in Congress, he would have to get rid of Cameron.

In late January, Lincoln replaced Cameron with Edwin Stanton, the attorney general in James Buchanan's administration.

Union General George McClellan

At the end of January 1862, Lincoln decided to prod the military into action. He called for the army and navy to make a general advance by February 22. General Ulysses S. Grant responded by launching a campaign to open up the Cumberland and Tennessee Rivers in northern Tennessee with the help of Flag Officer Andrew Foote and his navy gunboats. On February 6, Grant captured Fort Henry and eleven days later, Fort Donelson. On February 23, the Union Army of the Ohio, headed by Don Carlos Buell, pushed toward Nashville from the north, forcing the Rebels to evacuate. The Union now controlled all of Kentucky and most of Tennessee.

Union supporters were ecstatic. "The cause of the Union now marches on in every section of the country," the *New York Tribune* declared. "It now requires no very far-reaching prophet to predict the end of the struggle." Lincoln made the bold Ulysses S. Grant a major general. For the moment, no one was terribly upset that the Army of the Potomac was not moving.

In 1862, Lincoln appointed Andrew Johnson—the Unionist senator from Tennessee—as that state's military governor.

A Family Tragedy

The evening before Grant captured Fort Henry, the Lincolns gave a lavish party to show off the newly decorated White House. Five hundred guests, including senators, military officers, and Supreme Court justices, were invited. The Lincolns were elegantly dressed for the affair. The president wore a new black coat and Mary, a white silk dress covered with tiny black silk flowers. But they were too distracted to enjoy the party. Upstairs, Willie was sick with typhoid fever, which may have been caused by polluted drinking water in the White House.

The boy grew increasingly weak, and Lincoln stayed up nights bathing his face with cool water and giving medicine to Tad, who had a milder case. On February 20, Willie died. The president wandered into the office of Nicolay, his secretary. "Well, Nicolay, my boy is gone—he is actually gone," he said. Then, his face damp with tears, he went to tell Tad.

63

Lincoln grieved for a long time, occasionally shutting himself in a room to cry. But he was able to function. Mary was so stricken by grief that she remained in bed for weeks. Willie was her favorite, and she never again went into the room where he died.

Union Moves in the West

Despite Lincoln's call for a general advance, McClellan did not move against the enemy, but he did, at least, explain his strategy. The young general was determined to advance on Richmond, Virginia. Lincoln was doubtful. He realized that defeating the Confederate armies was much more important than the symbolic act of taking the Confederate capital. He urged McClellan to advance on the Confederates in Manassas, but the general insisted on Richmond. While he prepared for an advance, Lincoln reorganized the huge Army of the Potomac into four corps and put McClellan at the head. But he relieved him from his position as general-in-chief. McClellan would now be one of three generals reporting to Secretary of War Stanton.

★

In March 1862, Robert E. Lee was named military advisor to Jefferson Davis.

★

In late March 1862, Grant and about 45,000 men were moving up the Tennessee River. They expected to be joined by Buell and his 25,000 men, marching from Nashville. When the two armies were united, they would attack the Confederates in northern Mississippi.

64

Part of the battlefield near Shiloh Church, in Tennessee, where Union troops won a victory but lost nearly 13,000 men.

On April 6, Grant's men were camped near Shiloh Church in the town of Pittsburg Landing, close to the Mississippi border, when they were attacked by Confederates. The Federals were nearly pushed into the Tennessee River, but the next day, when Buell's men arrived, the tide turned. The price of the Union's victory was huge—almost 13,000 killed or wounded. Losses on the Confederate side were about the same. Grant's superior, Henry Halleck, blamed him for the shocking number of casualties and tried to remove him from his command, but Lincoln would not allow it. "I can't spare this man," Lincoln said. "He fights."

McClellan, in the meantime, began a slow campaign up the Virginia Peninsula with the capture of Richmond his goal. The general had

Abraham Lincoln

a tendency to greatly overestimate the numbers of his enemy, which made him overly cautious. In addition, his own troops had been hit hard by typhoid fever and malaria.

By mid-June, McClellan was finally outside of Richmond, but he never got the chance to attack. On June 25, the Confederates' new commander, Robert E. Lee, flung his troops at McClellan's army. In a series of struggles that became known as the Seven Days' battles, the Confederates forced McClellan back down the Peninsula.

The Emancipation Proclamation

Although Lincoln had made it clear that the preservation of the Union was uppermost in his mind, many African Americans hoped that the outbreak of the war would bring the end of slavery. As the war continued, thousands of slaves fled north to find freedom. Some made a rush for Union army lines, bringing valuable military information about the movement of Confederate troops. In Washington, meanwhile, calls for emancipation grew increasingly loud among congressmen who were frustrated with the performance of the Union army. They thought it would be more difficult for the Confederacy to continue the war if the slaves, who worked the farms while the whites served in the military, were emancipated.

At the beginning of the war, Lincoln had resisted ending slavery for a number of reasons. He felt that the Constitution did not give him the authority to outlaw slavery, even in the Confederate states, though he was convinced that slavery was wrong. In addition, he was afraid of angering slave holders in border states like Maryland and Missouri, because he was afraid they would join the Confederacy.

By June 1862, however, Lincoln had changed his mind about emancipation. McClellan's defeat on the Virginia Peninsula had damaged the Union's morale. It was time for a different military plan. The Constitution allowed him to end slavery for military reasons, and he now felt emancipation should be part of the Union's strategy.

Lincoln wrote the first draft of the Emancipation Proclamation during June and July. Instead of working on it in the White House, where he was often disturbed, he went to the telegraph office of the War Department, where he often awaited news from the army, and where he could work comfortably. Lincoln asked the officer in charge to guard his document, and came back every day to work on it.

On July 22, Lincoln read the first draft to his cabinet. He explained that it was time for stronger military measures, and that ending slavery in the Confederacy would be a major blow to the South. The Emancipation Proclamation would only apply to slaves in the Confederate states because the border states were not at war with the Union. It would take effect on January 1, 1863. Seward persuaded Lincoln to wait for a Union victory before

This fanciful painting shows Lincoln working on the Emancipation Proclamation.

issuing the proclamation, to ensure that it was viewed an act of strength and not desperation.

Another Encounter at Bull Run

Lincoln would have to wait for a Union victory. As usual, McClellan was not moving. At the end of August, Lincoln was more encouraged. General John Pope's Army of Virginia was again battling Lee's forces in Manassas, Virginia. The president haunted the telegraph office, hoping for news of a victory. Instead, on August 30, he learned that Lee had dealt the Union troops a mighty blow and sent them running back to

Washington. Upon hearing the news, he wandered into his secretary's room. "Well, John, we are whipped again."

Lee followed up on the Confederates' smashing victory by invading Maryland, which upset a great many Northerners. Lincoln's general-in-chief, Henry Halleck, insisted that McClellan should head a combined force of Pope's battered Army of Virginia and the Army of the Potomac to fight Lee's army. Reluctantly, Lincoln agreed. A storm of criticism rained down on Lincoln from his cabinet and from influential Republicans. Lincoln felt he had few alternatives; he was running out of good generals. But if McClellan defeated Lee's army in Maryland, he would announce his Emancipation Proclamation.

★

After his defeat at the second Bull Run, General Pope was sent to Minnesota to keep Native Americans under control.

★

President Lincoln had learned how to evaluate a military situation quickly without acting rashly. He was not yet comfortable managing his generals, however, who often seemed to ignore his wishes. Lincoln was clearly a very strong man, and even as he was grieving for his lost son, he continued to lead the nation through a brutal struggle. The first year and a half of the war also revealed Lincoln's practical side. Although he wished for an end to slavery with all of his heart, he turned to emancipation as a military solution for a war that was not going well.

69

Chapter 4

The Union victory that gave Lincoln the opportunity to move forward with emancipation, came on September 17 at Antietam Creek, near the town of Sharpsburg, Maryland. It was the bloodiest day in American history: 6,000 men were killed and another 17,000 were wounded. The victory itself was little more than a draw. The Union had gained scarcely a mile of land occupied by Rebels. Nevertheless, Lee's troops were battered, outnumbered, and in retreat. A quick strike from the North might have ended the war.

OPPOSITE: Union officers relax at a military camp in Virginia.

71

The next day, however, McClellan once again overestimated the size of his enemy. Even though two fresh Union divisions had arrived that morning, he did not try to deliver the final blow that would destroy Lee's army.

Although costly, Antietam was still a victory, and Lincoln released his proclamation. He read it to his cabinet on September 22, 1862. That evening the Government Printing Office worked late getting copies ready for the press and for government departments. Fifteen thousand copies would be distributed to various military commanders and their men. Lincoln would sign the final copy of the proclamation on New Year's Day, when it would take effect.

A Historic New Year's Day

On January 1, 1863, Lincoln and Mary went down to the Blue Room at 11 A.M. to host the annual New Year's Day party. Diplomats, army officers, and Washingtonians lined up to greet the president and the First Lady, who looked lovely in a silver silk dress. It was her first reception since Willie's death.

In the afternoon, Lincoln went upstairs to his office. With Secretary of State Seward and a few other cabinet ministers watching, he dipped a gold pen in a bottle of ink and prepared to sign the Emancipation Proclamation. After shaking so many hands at the reception down below, Lincoln found that his hand was trembling. He worried that a shaky signature might lead someone to believe he was having some doubts, when in fact, the opposite was true. "I never, in my life, felt more certain that I was doing right, than I do in signing this paper," he said.

The document freed all slaves in the Confederacy, except those in areas occupied by Union troops, regions no longer considered part of the Confederacy. With his signature, Lincoln declared that over three million slaves—men, women, and children—"are and henceforth shall be free."

Down the street from the White House, an African American preacher, Henry M. Turner, had someone read the proclamation to a group of African Americans, who responded by shouting, clapping, and singing. A crowd soon gathered outside the White House and called for Lincoln, who appeared at a window and bowed. Summing up the scene, Preacher Turner said in amazement, "Nothing like it will ever be seen again in this life."

★

Frederick Douglass called the Emancipation Proclamation "the answer to the agonizing prayer of centuries."

★

On that day and during the week that followed, there were large celebrations in many Northern cities. In Boston, 3,000 people gathered at the Tremont Street Temple on New Year's Day and waited anxiously until after eight in the evening for word that Lincoln had actually signed the document. When it finally came, shouts and sobs greeted the welcome news.

Not everyone was happy, of course. The proclamation did, indeed, convert the Civil War into a

This newspaper illustration celebrates the freedoms outlined and promised by the Emancipation Proclamation.

war for freedom. But its power to unite the North was not felt immediately. For months the president continued to be a scapegoat for the North's terrible morale. Some Republicans even wanted him removed from office. To escape his isolation and forget his troubles, Lincoln spent a lot of time with his son, Tad. He helped him train his dog and cat, and even allowed the young boy to interrupt his cabinet meetings when Tad needed help.

Defeat in Chancellorsville

Lincoln hoped that the spring of 1863 would bring much-needed victories and—if all went as planned—the collapse of the Confederacy. A major offensive was to take place on a number of fronts, from Virginia to the Mississippi Valley. For the first time, the Union army would include African American regiments.

On April 28, General Joseph "Fighting Joe" Hooker, the new commander of the Army of the Potomac, took his men into Virginia to strike at Lee's army. At Chancellorsville, a crossroads near Fredericksburg, however, Hooker seemed to lose his courage and did not press his attack on the Confederates. Lee sensed his advantage, and in spite of being outnumbered two-to-one, he sent Stonewall Jackson to strike Hooker first. The Union suffered 17,000 casualties and the Confederates 13,000. On May 5, Hooker and his forces retreated.

Lincoln, who had been hovering over the War Department's telegraph machine for days, waiting for news, learned of Hooker's defeat on May 6. A newspaperman noticed that the president's face turned white. "My God!" he exclaimed. "What will the country say?"

★

On May 2, Stonewall Jackson was accidently shot by his own men. He died on May 11.

★

There was no good military news from any other region to lessen the pain of Chancellorsville. The number of complaints against Lincoln's administration skyrocketed. Some Northerners even urged Lincoln to make peace with the Confederacy.

The Tide Turns

Early in the summer of 1863, Lee was again moving to the North. While this made many Washingtonians anxious, Lincoln knew it would be much easier to

75

Robert Todd Lincoln

★ ★ ★ ★ ★

Born in 1843, Robert Todd was the eldest of Lincoln's children and the only one to live to adulthood. As a child, he spent very little time with the president, who was often away from home. Robert developed into a much cooler and more aloof individual than his father, and the two were never close.

After graduating from Harvard College in 1864, Robert briefly attended Harvard Law School. When he expressed a strong wish to see the war before it was over, Lincoln consented, though Mary was very afraid of losing yet another son. Understanding the president's concerns, General Grant kept Robert out of danger by assigning him the job of escorting visitors to the Army of the Potomac.

After Lincoln's death, Robert moved to Chicago with Mary and Tad. Robert remained there for 46

fight Lee on Union soil. The Army of the Potomac would be the key player, once again. Hooker resigned in an argument with general-in-chief Halleck over strategy, and Lincoln happily replaced him with George Meade, an experienced corps years, becoming a prominent lawyer like his father. In 1868, Robert married Mary Eunice Harlan. The couple had three children: Mary; Abraham, who died while still a teenager; and Jessie.

In 1875, Robert arranged for an insanity hearing for his mother, who was committed to a mental institution for several months. By then, Tad had died of pleurisy and Mary had become very interested in the supernatural. Mary exhibited all kinds of strange behavior—she bought a dozen pairs of curtains when she had no house in which to hang them, for example. (She lived in a hotel.) But she was a danger to no one, and she never forgave Robert.

In 1881, Robert became President James Garfield's Secretary of War. Tragically, Garfield, like Robert's father, was assassinated while in office. He served under President Benjamin Harrison before taking a job with the Pullman Company until 1911. Robert was almost eighty-three when he died. At his wife's request, he was buried at Arlington Cemetery, rather than in the Lincoln tomb in Springfield.

commander in Hooker's army. Meade immediately followed Lee, who had entered Pennsylvania.

While Meade pursued Lee, General Grant had laid siege to Vicksburg, Mississippi. After a series of battles in the Mississippi Valley, Grant managed to

The Battle of Gettysburg in 1863 was the bloodiest battle of the Civil War. Lee's defeat dealt a critical blow to the Rebel army and made eventual victory possible for the North.

push the Rebels into the city. He and his men surrounded it with a network of trenches and bombarded the population with thousands of shells a day. As Grant's siege dragged on through June, the president waited anxiously, expecting Vicksburg to fall.

The president also worried about the fate of Meade's army in southern Pennsylvania. By July 1, he was receiving messages at the telegraph office that the Confederate and Union armies had finally met in the town of Gettysburg and were struggling for positions on the ridges south of the town. On July 3, Lincoln learned of Lee's massive assault on the front lines of the Union, which commanded the high ground. The Union pushed the Confederates back with a heavy barrage of fire, and the next day the Confederates were in retreat. The Union had won a great victory, but a very costly one: 23,000 Union casualties and 28,000 for the Confederates. It was the bloodiest battle in U.S. history.

Lincoln figured that Meade was now in a position to finish off Lee's army. While waiting for further news, Gideon Welles, the secretary of the Navy, came to tell Lincoln that the Confederates in Vicksburg surrendered to Grant. The Mississippi River belonged to the Union. Lincoln threw his arms around the secretary and said with a great smile, "What can we do for the secretary of the Navy for this glorious intelligence? He is always giving us good news."

A week later, Lincoln's joy returned to frustration. Meade had allowed Lee to retreat to Virginia. "We had them within our grasp," Lincoln sighed. "We had only to stretch forth our hands and they were ours." The war would go on for nearly two more years. Union victories in Vicksburg and Gettysburg, however, created a turning point for the war. These defeats cost the Confederates almost 60,000 troops, and they would never regain their full strength.

The Gettsyburg Address

For the rest of the summer and fall of 1863, the military front was fairly quiet. Early in November, Lincoln was invited to speak at the dedication of the new National Soldiers' Cemetery on the

79

Gettysburg battlefield, where thousands killed in the battle were being reburied. Although he had turned down similar requests to speak in the past, this time he agreed. The president had been looking for an opportunity to remind the nation of the purposes of the war—the reasons why so many people in the Union had made, and would continue to make, great sacrifices.

When Lincoln's train pulled into Gettysburg, hotels were overflowing with visiting dignitaries and relatives of soldiers killed at Gettysburg. The next morning was sunny, and the president rode a horse, which seemed far too short for his long legs, in a slow procession to the cemetery. He waited on a wooden platform while the main speaker, the white-haired Edward Everett, spoke for two hours. A much-admired speaker, Everett gave a moving description of the great battle, bringing some members of the audience to tears.

Lincoln followed with a short but powerful speech. He began by reminding his audience of the Declaration of Independence, which spelled out the principles on which the nation was founded. And he connected these principles with the Civil War.

> *Four score and seven years ago our fathers brought forth on this continent a new nation, conceived in Liberty, and dedicated to the proposition that all men are created equal.*
>
> *Now we are met in a great civil war, testing whether that nation or any nation so conceived and so dedicated*

Though Lincoln's address at Gettysburg was brief, it is remembered as his most famous and most powerful speech.

can long endure. It is . . . for us to be here dedicated to the great task remaining before us—that from these honored dead we take increased devotion to that cause for which they gave the last full measure of devotion—that we here highly resolve that these dead shall not have died in vain— that this nation, under God, shall have a new birth of freedom—-and that government of the people, by the people, for the people, shall not perish from earth.

Lincoln's speech was so short that his audience was startled to realize it was over. The president's ability to say so much with so few words is one of the wonders of the Gettysburg address. It is his most famous speech, and it has probably been more influential than any other in the nation's history.

81

Chapter 5

PEACE AND TRAGEDY

Lincoln returned from Gettysburg with a mild form of smallpox, a contagious disease, and was forced to remain in bed for three weeks. In a joking reference to all the job seekers who usually came to see him, Lincoln said he now had something to give everyone!

While still in bed, the president worked on his annual December address to Congress. Since the war seemed to be coming to an end, he proposed terms for amnesty and reconstruction—pardoning, reorganizing, and re-admitting the Confederate states into the Union. Lincoln favored generous terms, including a full pardon. But he also demanded proof of the Confederates' loyalty and their acceptance of the emancipation of slaves.

OPPOSITE: After Ulysses S. Grant became general-in-chief of all Union armies, he presented Lincoln with a plan for crushing the Rebels and ending the war.

83

Lincoln Finds the Right General

During the winter of 1864, Lincoln became increasingly frustrated with the Union's lack of progress. Since his failure to pursue Lee after Gettysburg, Meade seemed to have lost his nerve. Although the Army of the Potomac clashed with Lee's Army of Northern Virginia, there were no significant battles. Lincoln decided to bring a bold general, Ulysses S. Grant, east to become the general-in-chief of all Northern armies.

Grant arrived in Washington on March 8, just in time for a weekly reception given at the White House. At age forty-two, he was a slim man, not very tall, and not very talkative. Lincoln gave him a warm welcome. Everyone crowded around the general, who had to stand on a sofa to avoid being trampled while trying to shake hands with all the well wishers.

It was not long before Grant presented Lincoln with an overall military plan. On May 4, all the Union armies would begin major attacks on the Confederates at one time. In the East, under Grant's command, the Army of the Potomac would push Lee's men into Richmond while Union troops under Benjamin Butler would head towards Petersburg, Virginia, and then Richmond. In the Shenandoah Valley, Confederate rail lines would be destroyed. Farther west, William Tecumseh Sherman's Army of the Cumberland would move on Atlanta, and Nathaniel Banks' forces in Louisiana would attack Mobile, Alabama.

Lincoln was delighted with the plan. Since 1861, he had been urging the Union armies to use their advantage in numbers by making a major, coordinated advance. Ever the diplomat, Lincoln pretended Grant's was a fresh idea, and expressed great pleasure at his strategy.

Heavy Losses

The Union's great offensive began when Grant's army of 115,00 struck Lee's 64,000 men in the Wilderness, a densely wooded region southwest of Washington. A few days later, Grant met Lee's forces again in Spotsylvania, to the south, where he could not break Lee's line. In these two battles, fought between March 5 and March 12, Grant's army suffered 32,000 casualties, and Lee's 18,000. Grant was becoming frustrated. On June 3, he ordered his exhausted men to launch a massive assault on the Confederates at Cold Harbor, east of Richmond. The Rebels, who were now fighting a defensive war, fought from their trenches. The Union suffered 7,000 casualties in one day; the Confederates, 1,500.

The enormous loss of life sickened Northerners. Lincoln tried to boost the Union's sinking morale, but in private, he was greatly pained by the continued bloodshed and was not able to sleep.

Grant's Plan Unravels

The general-in-chief's grand plan seemed to be coming apart. On June 14, after an unsuccessful assault on Petersburg, Grant changed his strategy. He decided to lay siege to the city so Lee's forces would not be able to leave and help the Confederates in Georgia fight Sherman. Lincoln was disappointed; but he wired Grant to "hold on with bull dog grip and chew & choke as much as possible."

Meanwhile, Butler's army was trapped in Virginia, and Union men in the Shenandoah Valley met with little success. In the West, Union forces were unable to launch an offensive against Mobile, Alabama. And in Georgia, Sherman was having trouble pushing the Confederates toward Atlanta.

The Election of 1864

The Republican national convention in Baltimore was dominated by Lincoln supporters who got the president a unanimous nomination. For vice president, the delegates nominated Andrew Johnson, a Southerner and a War Democrat—a Democrat who supported Lincoln's war aims.

Despite his party's encouraging vote, Lincoln was not at all sure he would win a second term in the November election. The Union's enormous number of casualties—about 100,000 since Grant began his campaign in May—was weakening Northern support for the war. To make matters worse, in early July, almost 15,000 Confederates managed to get within five miles of the White House.

Lincoln went out to Fort Stevens the next day to watch the fighting from a balcony. He seemed untroubled by the bullets whizzing over his stovepipe hat.

In an 1864 campaign poster, Lincoln, left, shakes hands with a workman while former slaves run free. On the right, McClellan shakes hands with Jefferson Davis at a slave auction.

The presence of Confederate troops so close to Washington certainly did not win Lincoln support for the upcoming election. If anything, it encouraged those in the Union urging Lincoln to negotiate a peace agreement. Many of them were War Democrats. They wanted Lincoln to abandon his goal of emancipation and make peace with the Confederates if they would join the Union. Lincoln refused to compromise. By then, about 100,000 African Americans were fighting in the Union army and navy. "If they stake their lives for us," Lincoln said, "they must be prompted by the strongest motive—even the promise of freedom. And the promise being made, must be kept." At the end of August, the Democrats nominated the former Union commander George McClellan for president. McClellan was supposed to support the party's platform, which claimed the war was a failure and called for an immediate negotiated peace settlement. The general could not condemn the war, and in the end, he didn't support the platform. Once again,

Lincoln stuck with tradition and did not publicly campaign for himself. Nor did he comment on the Democrats' campaign literature, which was frequently outrageous.

On September 2, Lincoln—and the Union—got the "great change" that was urgently needed. Sherman forced the Confederates to surrender Atlanta, pushing them farther south. Lincoln was now the commander-in-chief of a winning army, and the Republicans united behind him.

Election Day, November 8, was dreary and rainy. Lincoln spent it waiting anxiously for the final count. In the evening he settled down in the War Room's telegraph office with John Hay and some others. By midnight, when they were sharing a supper of fried oysters, Lincoln knew he had won. Once he was in bed, his friend Ward Lamon, the U.S. marshal for Washington, D. C., quietly planted himself outside Lincoln's room. Lamon was afraid that, with Lincoln's second term assured, an angry Southerner would try to assassinate the president.

Sherman's March to the Sea

The week after Lincoln's re-election, General William Tecumseh Sherman began a new phase of the Civil War. He decided to ignore the Confederates he had chased out of Atlanta. His plan was to march through the heart of Georgia to the sea, destroying factories, railroads, and farms— anything that helped the Confederates fight.

Eventually, Sherman wanted to come up on Lee's rear in Virginia. In the meantime, he hoped to break the will of the Southerners to continue the war. Like Lincoln, Sherman believed in a tough war and generous terms for peace. Now the fight was directed against civilians as well as soldiers. Lincoln and Grant were uncomfortable with Sherman's plan, but they had given him their blessings.

The president worried about the safety of his general, who was out of touch with him for long periods of time. "I know the hole he went in at," he told a visitor, "but I can't tell you what hole he'll come out of." Finally, on December 22, 1864 he received Sherman's telegram: "I beg to present you, as a Christmas gift, the city of Savannah, with 150 guns and plenty of ammunition."

The Thirteenth Amendment

Lincoln was especially pleased by Sherman's news because he was involved in difficult negotiations with members of the House of Representatives The president wanted Congress to approve the Thirteenth Amendment to the Constitution, which would abolish slavery in the United States. The Emancipation Proclamation only applied to the Confederate states, not the border states. Lincoln was afraid it might some day be declared an illegal use of presidential power. The amendment had already been approved by the Senate, and Lincoln

89

was anxious for it to pass in the House before his inauguration. Then it would have to be ratified by a popular vote.

The congressional vote took place on January 31, 1865. After the roll call, a clerk read the results: 119 congressmen voted to ratify, and 58 voted against. The required two-thirds majority had been exceeded by three votes. The chamber came back to life with a jolt. Some Republican congressmen hugged one another, others cried, and spectators cheered. Outside, cannons boomed in a 100-gun salute. African Americans gathered together in great numbers to celebrate.

A Second Term Begins

Lincoln's second inauguration took place on March 4, 1865. By then, Columbia, the capital of South Carolina, had fallen to Sherman's troops They were continuing northward toward Richmond.

African Americans celebrate the passage of the Thirteenth Amendment to the Constitution, which ended slavery.

As Lincoln stepped forward to give his Second Inaugural Address in front of the Capitol, the sun burst through layers of clouds. In his speech, which many regard as one of his finest, the president again touched upon the causes of the war. Without heaping blame on the Southerners, Lincoln said simply, "Both parties deprecated war, but one of them would make war rather than let the nation survive, and the other would accept war rather than let it perish, and the war came." God punished the North and South with a long war, Lincoln continued, because both were to blame for 250 years of slavery in the United States. He brought his speech to a ringing conclusion by describing the generous spirit that he hoped would characterize the reconstruction:

With malice toward none, with charity for all, with firmness in the right as God gives us to see the right, let us strive on to finish the work we are in, to bind up the nation's wounds, to care for him who shall have borne the battle and for his widow and his orphan, to do all which may achieve and cherish a just and lasting peace among ourselves and with all nations.

Frederick Douglass, the African American abolitionist, came to the White House that evening to attend Lincoln's inaugural reception. Police stopped him at the door, but Lincoln had him shown in at once. He had consulted Douglass on many occasions. Now he welcomed

91

him warmly, calling him "my old friend, Douglass."
Lincoln said, "I saw you in the crowd today
listening to my address. There is no man in the
country whose opinion I value more than yours.
I want to know what you think of it." Douglass
voiced his approval, to Lincoln's obvious delight.

The War Speeds to Conclusion

By the end of March, Lee realized that he would
have to escape Grant and leave Petersburg or
Sherman would soon arrive and trap him. The
Confederate general knew that his departure also
meant that Richmond would fall, but he felt he
had no choice. On March 25, Lee ordered a
successful surprise attack on the Union forces at
Fort Stedman, east of Petersburg. Grant's men
immediately counterattacked, and regained the
ground they had lost. Then, on March 29, Grant
ordered a coordinated attack on Lee's forces. Lee
fled south and, on April 1, Richmond fell.

Lincoln wanted to visit the former capital of the
Confederacy. On April 4, he and Tad were rowed
into Richmond on a barge, with Admiral David
Porter at the helm. Holding Tad's hand, Lincoln
walked through the ruined city accompanied by
ten sailors and Admiral Porter. The admiral
looked nervously through every window for a
potential assassin. This became increasingly
difficult as masses of former slaves enthusiastically
surrounded the president.

On April 9, the president learned that Lee had surrendered at Appamatox Courthouse. Other Confederate armies would soon follow his example.

Early the next morning, cannons boomed the news to everyone within earshot and in the process, broke some windows in Lafayette Square. Later, about 3,000 people followed a brass band up to the White House. When they called for the president, Tad first appeared at a balcony and was cheered enthusiastically. Lincoln showed himself briefly and promised a speech the next night.

President Lincoln was greeted by masses of former slaves as he walked through the streets of Richmond with his son, Tad.

The next night, greeted by cheers, the president read a speech, commenting on the joyful occasion and expressing the nation's thanks to General Grant and his brave officers and men. Among the crowd was someone who did not join the cheers.

John Wilkes Booth, a handsome, twenty-six-year-old actor from Maryland, was furious. When he heard Lincoln talk of giving African American men the vote, Booth vowed that Lincoln would never give another speech.

Booth had been plotting against Lincoln for more than six months and had recruited six men to help him. At first, the co-conspirators planned to kidnap Lincoln and hold him hostage until thousands of Confederate soldiers were released from Northern prisons. On at least two occasions, Lincoln unknowingly evaded the men by making last-minute changes in his schedule.

John Wilkes Booth was at the center of the plot to assassinate the president.

By March, Booth had become frustrated. After hearing Lincoln's speech, he made definite plans for an assassination. Three out of his six original partners agreed to help.

The plan was, while Booth murdered the president, his co-conspirator Lewis Paine would kill Secretary of State Seward. Booth's reasoning was that Seward would be the one to organize new elections in the North. David Herold, a young druggist's clerk who was familiar with the streets of Washington, was going to escort Paine to Seward's Home. Meanwhile, George Atzerodt would murder vice president Andrew Johnson.

On April 14, Good Friday, Lincoln met with his cabinet to discuss how the Confederate states would be integrated into the Union. As always, Lincoln wanted to offer generous terms, and his cabinet agreed. Stanton was impressed with Lincoln's command of the meeting.

★

U.S. Grant and his wife were supposed to accompany the Lincolns to the theater that night, but cancelled.

★

In the afternoon, the president took a carriage ride with Mary. He seemed so happy that Mary said, "Dear Husband, you almost startle me with your cheerfulness." That evening, they planned to go Ford's Theater to see a play, despite the warnings of Lincoln's advisers. Stanton thought Lincoln should resist mingling with theater crowds. Lincoln thought his advisers were being overly cautious.

The president loved going to the theatre. Shakespeare was his favorite playwright, and Lincoln almost never missed a chance to see one of his tragedies performed. He also liked comedies, and was looking forward to seeing *Our American Cousin*, which was full of corny humor.

On the way to the theater, the Lincolns picked up Clara Harris, the daughter of a New York

95

The president was attending a performance of *Our American Cousin* at Ford's Theater on the night he was killed.

senator, and her fiancé, Major Henry Rathbone, who would join them in the box where the Lincolns always sat. They were late, and the play had already begun. Spotting the president as he entered the theater, the orchestra leader interrupted the play with "Hail to the Chief," which was, and still is, played for the president of the United States on ceremonial occasions. The audience stood and cheered.

By the third act, Booth had made his way to Lincoln's box. The Washington policeman in charge of guarding it had left his post, and Booth was two feet from the president's chair. Onstage, an actor delivered one of the funniest lines in the play, when suddenly a gunshot rang out in the theater and Lincoln slumped over. Major

96

Rathbone tried to grab Booth, who stabbed him with a hunting knife. Booth leapt onto the stage, catching the spur of his boot on a flag that decorated the presidential box, and broke the bone above his ankle. After shouting in Latin *"Sic semper tyranus!"* ("Thus Be It Ever to Tyrants!") Booth limped away. No one was sure what had happened until Mary screamed, "They have shot the president!"

An army surgeon, Charles Leale, examined Lincoln. Detecting a slight pulse, he had the president moved to a house across the street that belonged to a tailor, William Petersen. There, Lincoln's long frame lay diagonally across a mattress that was too small for him.

Secretary of War Stanton took charge, setting up headquarters at a back parlor in Petersen's home. He soon learned that Booth was the assailant, and that someone else had tried to

Booth was less than two feet from the president when he fired the fatal shot.

kill Seward, who was still alive. Stanton ordered a massive hunt for the attackers.

As the night wore on, all the members of the cabinet came to see the president, except Seward. Several doctors watched over the president. Mary,

97

The Ride Home: Lincoln's Funeral Train

Lincoln's death produced an enormous outpouring of grief throughout much of the nation. In Washington, thousands of soldiers and ordinary citizens marched in a funeral procession from the White House to the Capitol on April 19. Many more filed past the president's coffin the next day.

On April 21, Lincoln's casket was placed on a nine-car funeral train bound for Springfield. Decorated with Union flags, the train retraced much of the journey he took when he traveled to Washington as a president-elect. Willie's casket, removed from a cemetery in Washington, was on the train as well. In cities along the 1,600-mile route, Lincoln's casket was placed in public buildings so people could pay their respects. In

beside herself with grief, tried desperately to get her husband to speak to her.

Lincoln never regained consciousness, and died at 7:22 A.M. on April 15, nine hours after he was shot. Stanton, his face damp with tears, said solemnly, "Now he belongs to the angels."

Philadelphia, the coffin was laid in Independence Hall, where the Declaration of Independence had been signed. In New York City, about 85,000 people followed the funeral carriage. Some watched from windows, including future president, Theodore Roosevelt, who was then a six-year-old boy. The funeral train finally reached Springfield on May 3. The next day, mourners laid bouquets on Lincoln's coffin, thus beginning the American custom of flowers at a funeral.

Tens of thousands marched in Lincoln's funeral procession in Washington, D.C.

Lewis Paine and George Atzerodt were arrested the morning that Lincoln died. Booth managed to avoid capture until April 26, when he and an accomplice were found hiding in a barn on a Virginia farm. Booth resisted arrest and was shot to death by Stanton's men.

Epilogue

Lincoln's assassination robbed the nation of perhaps its greatest president. His quiet strength and compassionate leadership were sorely missed

during the difficult period of reconstruction after the Civil War.

Perhaps Abraham Lincoln's most lasting legacy is the enduring eloquence of his speeches. No other president since has been able to match the simple power and beauty of the Gettysburg Address or the Second Inaugural Address, both of which are carved into the Lincoln Memorial in Washington, D.C. These words gave the people of a war-weary Union the sense that they shared truly important goals and inspired them to support the war that would ultimately prevent their great nation from being "a house divided against itself."

The Lincoln Memorial, Washington, D.C.

Abraham Lincoln

Glossary

abolitionism A political movement in the 1800s that sought to ban slavery. Abolitionists worked for abolition.

amendment A change to a written document such as the U.S. Constitution.

assassinate To murder by sudden or secret attack.

compromise A settlement reached by mutual agreement of two opposing sides on an issue.

debate A discussion of opposing opinions regarding an issue.

division A military grouping of between 6,000 and 8,000 soldiers or two to three brigades.

emancipation Freedom.

malice Anger or vengeance.

plantation A large farm in the South worked by slaves in the years before the Civil War.

prejudice A negative opinion toward individuals or people of a different race, religion, social class, or other group.

Reconstruction The reorganization and reestablishment of the seceded states in the Union after the American Civil War.

secession Formal withdrawal from an organization.

siege A military strategy of keeping a force surrounded and unable to obtain food and arms to force a surrender.

territory A region of land that is not a state, but that has its own government.

typhoid fever A disease that causes fever, diarrhea, headache, and intestinal inflammation.

Whig A member or supporter of an American political party formed in 1834 in opposition to the Jacksonian Democrats, who were succeeded around 1854 by the Republican party.

101

For More Information

Web sites

Abraham Lincoln Research Site
http://members.aol.com/RVSNorton/Lincoln2.html
This web site includes a biography, photographs, and lots of information about Abraham Lincoln.

Abraham Lincoln online
http://showcase.netins.net/web/creative/lincoln.html
A complete resource for information with a "This date in Lincoln's life" feature as well as little known facts about Lincoln.

Abraham Lincoln: An Educational Site
http://www.geocities.com/SunsetStrip/Venue/5217/lincoln.html
A student-produced site with biographical information about Lincoln as well as links to the Civil War.

Lincoln Home National Historic Site
http://www.nps.gov/liho/home/home.htm
A National Park Service site with a virtual tour of the Springfield house and many links to other information about the Lincoln family.

Books

Donald, David. *Lincoln*. New York: Touchstone, 1996.

Gross, Ruth. *True Stories About Abraham Lincoln*. New York: Scholastic, 1991.

North, Sterling. *Abe Lincoln: Log Cabin to White House.* New York: Random Books, 1987.

Oates, Stephen. *Abraham Lincoln: The Man Behind the Myths*. New York, Harper, 1994.

Index

Anderson, Robert, 57

Bates, Edward, 55
Bell, John, 49
Berry, William, 17
Black Hawk War, 16–17
Blair, Montgomery, 56
Booth, John Wilkes, 94–97
Breckinridge, John C., 49
Brown, John, 38
Buchanon, James, 49, 56

Cameron, Simon, 56, 61
Chase, Salmon P., 55
Clay, Henry, 19, 29

Davis, Jefferson, 54, 58
Debates, 42
Douglas, Stephen A., 20, 24, 38, 42, 49, 56

Emancipation Proclamation, 69, 72–74, 89

Fort Sumter, 57

Gettysburg Address, 80–81, 100
Grant, Ulysses S., 62–63, 64, 84–86
Green, Bowling, 16

Hamlin, Hannibal, 49

Harrison, William Henry, 26
Herndon, Billy, 29
Hooker, Joseph "Fighting Joe", 75

Jackson, Andrew, 18–19
Johnson, Andrew, 86

Kansas-Nebraska Act, 36–38, 41

Lincoln & Herndon, 34, 51
Lincoln, Eddie, 30
Lincoln, Mary Todd, 26–28, 55, 64, 72, 95
Lincoln, Nancy, 12–13
Lincoln, Robert Todd, 28, 55, 76
Lincoln, Sarah, 12–13
Lincoln, Sarah Bush, 14
Lincoln, Tad, 34, 55, 61, 92
Lincoln, Thomas, 12, 34
Lincoln, William, 34, 55, 61, 63
Logan, Stephen T., 28–29
Long Nine, 21

McDowell, Irvin, 59
McClellan, George B., 59, 61, 64–69, 72, 87
Meade, George, 76–79
Missouri Compromise, 30–31, 36

Patterson, Robert, 59

Polk, James, 32

Seward, William, 45, 48, 55–56, 72, 97
Scott, Winfield, 58–59, 61
Sherman, William Tecumseh, 88–89
Stanton, Edwin, 62
Stuart & Lincoln, 24

Stuart, John Todd, 19, 24, 28

Taylor, Zachary, 33

Van Buren, Martin, 20, 33

Welles, Gideon, 56, 79
Wilmot, David, 33

Abraham Lincoln